California Natural Hi...

D0747175

NATIVE TREES

OF THE
SAN FRANCISCO BAY REGION

BY

WOODBRIDGE METCALF

ILLUSTRATED BY MARY B. AND FRED POMEROY
AND EUGENE MURMAN

UNIVERSITY OF CALIFORNIA PRESS
BERKELEY, LOS ANGELES, LONDON

CALIFORNIA NATURAL HISTORY GUIDES

General Editor: Arthur C. Smith

UNIVERSITY OF CALIFORNIA PRESS
BERKELEY AND LOS ANGELES, CALIFORNIA
UNIVERSITY OF CALIFORNIA PRESS, LTD.
LONDON, ENGLAND
© 1959 BY THE REGENTS OF THE UNIVERSITY OF CALIFORNIA

ISBN 0-520-00853-7
LIBRARY OF CONGRESS CATALOG CARD NUMBER: 59-6054
PRINTED IN THE UNITED STATES OF AMERICA

7 8 9 0

CONTENTS

ILLUSTRATION ON COVER
    Coast Redwood (*Sequoia sempervirens*)

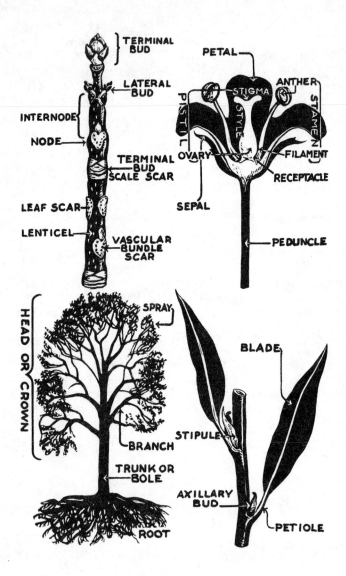

INTRODUCTION

When you look from almost any vantage point in the ten-county area surrounding San Francisco Bay, you realize that trees are notable features of the landscape. They not only contribute beauty as individual specimens, groves, or forests, but also add greatly to the comfort of both humans and animals. Some of the finest timber and ornamental trees in North America and some of the largest, oldest, and most beautiful trees in the world are found in this area, and you will find it a rewarding experience to make their acquaintance.

This central coast country, north through Sonoma County and south through Santa Cruz County, is a meeting ground for many tree species from the north Pacific Coast that reach their southern limit in the bay region and others from southern California that reach their northern limit here. Then, too, there are many trees in this region that have been introduced from all over the world. In the *Introduction to the Natural History of the San Francisco Bay Region*— the first volume of this series—there is a description of each of the region's sixteen biotic communities. Seven of these are forest communities, and trees are very important constituents of three others. Even in the grassland communities there are usually isolated tree specimens, and it is a rare chaparral community that does not contain at least a few trees.

You can add greatly to your interest and pleasure in traveling about this region by learning to recognize at least the more important trees. This book is designed to aid you in identifying the 52 native tree species.

The species accounts are brief, describing the trees and giving information on their range, habitat, and importance to man. Included also is a section on nature activities that can provide added pleasure and information. On page 71 is a check list of all native trees found in the bay region.

Black-and-white illustrations are by Mary B. and Fred Pomeroy; color illustrations are by Eugene Murman. Both the author and publisher wish to express their thanks to Dr. Lawrence Clark Powell and the University of California Library, Los Angeles, for permission to reproduce in reduced form the Murman watercolor drawings, which are part of a special collection of that library.

WHAT IS A TREE?

A tree is usually defined as a woody plant with a single upright stem, usually unbranched for some distance above the ground, reaching at maturity a height of 15 to 20 feet. However, several willows are usually included because of their size although they may have several stems from the same roots. A few species (*Ceanothus, Manzanita*) in this area are excluded because they rarely become larger than shrubs in the chaparral.

IDENTIFYING TREES

Trees have scientific and common names. The scientific name indicates the genus and species of each tree. (For a discussion of the method and purpose of naming plants, see *Introduction to the Natural History of the San Francisco Bay Region*, p. 18.) For example, Ponderosa Pine (*Pinus ponderòsa*) and Coast Live Oak (*Quercus agrifòlia*) are classified as follows:

Class Gymnospermae	Class Angiospermae
Subclass Polycotyledonae	Subclass Dicotyledonae
Order Coniferales	Order Fagales
Family Pinaceae	Family Fagaceae
Genus *Pinus*	Genus *Quercus*
Species *ponderòsa*	Species *agrifòlia*

For our purposes, we will consider trees of this area of mild climate in three groups, according to their leaf characteristics: one group—conifers—from the class Gymnospermae, and two groups—broadleaf evergreens and broadleaf deciduous—from the class Angiospermae.

In general, conifers are evergreen trees distinguished by their simple, needle-like or scale-like leaves. California has more native conifers than any region of similar size in the world, and many of them are native to the bay region.

Broadleaf evergreens are those trees which keep all or most of their leaves (usually leathery in texture) throughout the year.

Broadleaf deciduous are those trees from which the leaves (usually thinner and less leathery) fall in autumn, leaving the branches bare of foliage during the winter months.

An excellent place to test your ability to identify trees, and at the same time to observe some trees of striking beauty, is Golden Gate Park in San Francisco, Lake Merritt Park in Oakland, the University of California campus at Berkeley, or the Stanford University campus near Palo Alto. Many of the specimens in these tree collections are labeled. There are approximately 250 tree species on the campus at Berkeley, and even more are to be seen at Golden Gate Park where, in Strybing Arboretum, many are grouped according to country of origin. The botanical garden in Tilden Park in the Berkeley Hills has young specimens of native trees grouped according to forest provinces in California.

Identifying Introduced Trees

Since 1850, literally hundreds of tree species have been brought to this area from different parts of the world to line our streets and highways, for windbreaks and shade on farms, and for use as ornamentals in parks and home gardens. These introduced species, many of which are trees of outstanding beauty and charm, now greatly outnumber the natives. Some have escaped cultivation and can be found growing wild in various parts of the bay region. Because some of the introduced trees are similar in major characteristics to one or more of the native species, identification is sometimes difficult. If you should find a tree that you cannot identify with the information given in this book, it may be necessary either to consult one of the more detailed manuals listed on page 71 or to seek the assistance of an expert. If you obtain a good leaf, flower, or fruit specimen, your local county farm advisor, botany teacher, or one of the members of the local garden club can help you to identify the tree in question.

For more information on introduced trees, see *Ornamental Trees* (University of California Press) by Evelyn Maino and Frances Howard.

ACTIVITIES

In addition to observing and learning to recognize trees, there are many nature activities that can add greatly to your knowledge and pleasure.

GROWING TREES FROM SEED

This project involves a whole series of activities—including collection, extraction, and testing of seed; preparation of seedbed or flats; sowing the seed; and watering, weeding, and caring for the plants until they are ready for transplanting or setting out. You can get detailed information on all phases of this operation from University of California extension publications. If you have an opportunity, visit a nursery and observe how they handle and care for trees, shrubs, and other plants.

MAKING A HERBARIUM

If you are interested in making a herbarium, you can collect specimens of leaves, flowers, twigs, and fruits on your field trips. These specimens should be dried between folded newspapers or blotters and then mounted on cards giving the name of the species and the location and date of collection. This record, or collection of dried species, is called a herbarium. Botanical institutions around the world have been collecting specimens for more than a hundred years, preserving the records of famous botanical explorers.

MAKING A WOOD COLLECTION

If you can obtain permission to visit a lumber yard or construction project, you can usually find out from the carpenters the different types of wood being used and what they are being used for. Carpenters on construction projects and at lumber yards will often give you small samples of different types of wood. You can cut your wood specimens to a given size and shape, smooth them with sandpaper on all sides, and, if you wish, paint them with shellac or clear lacquer. If you carefully examine your specimens with a hand lens, you will soon be able to recognize a number of woods by their cross sections. Some collectors use a lathe to make small bowls or other woodcraft objects to add to the interest of their collection.

Making A Tree Census In Your Locality

You can become an "expert" on the trees in your neighborhood, in a park area, or in a certain country-side by making a map record. All you need is a map of the area—you can draw it yourself if one is not available—on which you can indicate by numbers the position of different trees. All trees of the same species should be given the same number. The map should also have a key or legend listing the numbers and the corresponding tree names.

Measuring Trees

It is interesting and easy to determine the height and diameter of certain favorite trees. On a sunny day the height of a tree that stands on fairly level ground can be determined by relating the length of its shadow to the shadow of a staff of known height. Thus if a staff 5 feet tall casts a shadow 3.5 feet long, the height of a tree that casts a shadow 50 feet long can be figured from the following proportion. The staff shadow is to the height of the staff as the tree shadow is to the height of the tree. Hence 3.5 : 5 as 50 : x, or 3.5 x = 250. Therefore x (the height of the tree) equals 71.4 feet.

A standard ruler marked in inches can be used as a hypsometer (instrument for measuring height) in the following way. Measure on the ground to a distance of 25 feet from the tree. Standing at this point, hold the ruler vertically at arms length (25 inches), with the zero point of the ruler on a line from your eye to the base of the tree. Then "sight" along the ruler to the top of the tree. Note the reading at the point where the line of sight intersects the ruler scale. If the line of sight intersects the ruler scale at 20.5 inches, the tree is 20.5 feet tall. For a taller tree, mark off a distance 50 feet from the base of the tree and double the reading on the ruler.

To determine the diameter of a tree, measure the circumference of the tree at 4.5 feet above ground. The circumference divided by pi (3.1416) gives the diameter.

MAKING A TREE CALENDAR

To make a tree calendar, select a tree (or two) near your home and keep a careful record of its growth and development throughout a year. First, you should do some preliminary investigation—learn about the species, genus, family, order, and class to which the tree belongs. With this information, you will gain some idea of what to expect during the year.

Your record should be based on careful observations of conditions and changes. You will wish to make a complete record of the height, trunk diameter, crown diameter, condition of foliage, exact location, and conditions around the tree. If you cannot find out when the tree was planted, you can at least make an estimate of its age. Are there dead branches, scars on the trunk, indications that the crown has been pruned, bird or animal nests in the crown, or evidence of insect or animal activity in or under the tree?

You will wish to notice the following things: when do the flowers appear, and are they of one or of two kinds; do insects work on the flowers, or is pollination accomplished by the wind; when does the fruit ripen; when do the seeds fall, and how are they distributed.

Collect a few seeds from a cone or fruit and see if you can estimate how many seeds will be produced by the tree during the year. When does leaf fall begin, and on what date is it fully completed? Even the "evergreen" species shed some of their leaves during the year. Did the tree show evidence of attack by insects or disease during the year, and did it require spraying or other treatment? Was there any damage by wind, frost, flooding, heat, or drought?

At the end of the year, write up a story of the tree from the facts gathered in your tree calendar. Good photographs or drawings of the tree, bark, leaves, flowers, and fruit will add interest to the story.

Growing Your Own Christmas Tree

If you have a six-foot-square open space in your yard, you can grow your own Christmas tree. A seedling Monterey Pine, Bishop Pine, Douglas Fir, or White Fir from a nearby nursery will grow into a symmetrical tree ready for cutting in from four to six years. The Monterey Pine and Bishop Pine grow fastest, Douglas Fir is intermediate, and the White Fir is the slowest-growing tree of the four species. If you have enough space to plant four or five trees, you can supply the family with a Christmas tree each year by planting one or two each spring. You can prune and trim the trees to the desired shape and thickness. For information on planting, caring for, and shaping these trees, see your county farm advisor or the extension forester at the University of California. The whole family can share in the pleasure of watching the trees grow and can join in the ceremony of cutting and setting up the tree. As the tree can be cut when needed, it will be fresh for the entire holiday season.

CALIFORNIA PLACE NAMES FROM TREES

With any available map of California, see how many place names based on trees that you can find. Make a list of these and indicate in which county each is located. You will easily recognize such names as Oakland, Redwood City, and Walnut Grove, but others may prove to be more difficult. You may have to look up Spanish names, such as Sausalito, Los Alamos, and Paso Robles. Erwin G. Gudde's book, *California Place Names,* which is available in your local library, will be of help in making your list.

RECOGNIZING TREES AT A DISTANCE

Alone or with companions you can enjoy the "game" of identifying trees from a distance. Observe a tree from a distance of a hundred yards or more and try to identify it from its general appearance and silhouette. After you have made your "guess," go up and compare the tree's characteristics with those described in this book to verify your identification. Trying to recognize trees from a distance will sharpen your powers of observation.

LOCATING TREES DESCRIBED IN THIS BOOK

You will find it a real challenge to locate specimens of all the trees described in this book. Take this book with you on your trips in the bay region, and write in the margin on the appropriate page the location of each tree, the date you found it, a few facts about its size, condition, and associates.

CONIFEROUS TREES

The bay region trees in this group have resinous, evergreen leaves that are needle-like (pines and firs), linear and flattened (redwood, yew, and nutmeg), or finely scale-like (cedars, cypresses, and mature junipers). The flowers are simple in structure, the two sexes occurring in tiny separate cones but usually on the same tree. The female flower bears the ovules exposed on the face of each scale, and fertilization is accomplished by wind-blown pollen grains that are yellow in color, dust-like in size, and produced in vast quantities by the male, or staminate, flowers.

The fruit is generally a woody cone with two or more winged seeds per cone scale, though on some trees, such as the junipers, the cone scales combine to form a berry containing one or more wingless, hard-shelled seeds. Yew and nutmeg fruits are also single seeded, but become succulent and berry-like or olive-like when mature.

Conifer wood is classed as softwood because it is composed of simple cells, called tracheids. Although the wood of most conifers is resinous and light, it is strong, seasons easily with little waste, and responds so well to shaping with tools that it is the most useful of all the woods of the world.

The great size of several of the conifers and the density (amount of timber per acre) of many forest stands are the basis for the vast lumber industry of the three Pacific Coast states. With better forest fire protection, increased skill in reforestation, and continuous forest management, there can be continued high production of lumber and other wood products from these forest areas.

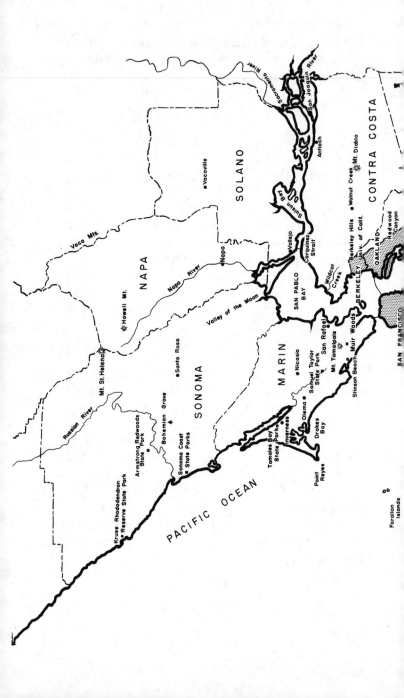

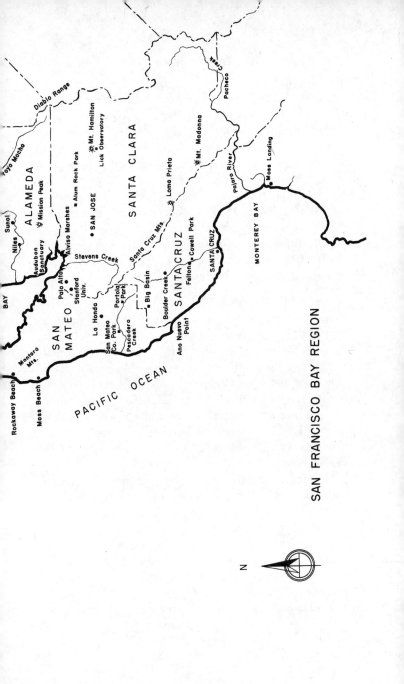

SAN FRANCISCO BAY REGION

The pines are distinguished from all other conifers by their slender, needle-like leaves that occur in bundles of 1 to 5, enclosed at the base by a sheath of papery scales. Their cones ripen during the second autumn, and are heavier and more woody than those of most other conifers. Borne two to a cone scale, the winged seeds usually fall after ripening. However, the cones of the three closed-cone species in this area— Monterey, Bishop, and Knobcone—remain unopened for some years after ripening. This is probably a means of insuring reforestation after fire, for the cones open after being heated. (For color illustrations of species of the pine family, see plates 1–3.)

Sugar Pine (*Pinus lambertiàna*)

One of the largest and most stately timber trees of the world, the Sugar Pine occasionally reaches a diameter of 10 ft. and a height of 250 ft. The long, horizontal branches with pendent, pitch-encrusted cones at their tips make these mighty trees veritable "towers of jewels" in the sun. On scars near the base of large trees, the pitch often crystallizes into white, sugary masses, said to have been used as a cathartic by the Indians. A white pine, its wood is soft, easily worked, and of high quality.

Unfortunately, this pine is threatened by White Pine Blister Rust, a serious disease that has wiped out both eastern and western white pines in many areas. Control is carried on by the removal of the disease's alternate hosts, various species of currant and gooseberry, from some of the most notable Sugar Pine stands. However, the natural range of this tree will probably be reduced by this disease.

Leaves and fruit: The blue-green, needle-like leaves,

[18]

2 to 4 in. long, are in bundles of fives. The cones hang from long stalks, are 15 to 20 in. long, and the cone scales are without prickles.

Range: The Sugar Pine grows to enormous size in the Sierra and Cascade ranges. In the bay region, Sugar Pine is found only in northern Sonoma County and on the higher slopes of Mount St. Helena where some specimens have survived successive fires. It does not take kindly to cultivation and is rarely seen as an ornamental. No other five-needled pine is native in this area, and the only one commonly seen in cultivation is the Bhotan Pine *(P. griffithi)* from the Himalaya Mountains in India.

Ponderosa Pine *(Pinus ponderòsa)*

Sometimes called Western Yellow Pine, this is the most widely distributed and important timber pine in the mountain forests of the coastal and Rocky Mountain states. The wood is fine grained, easily worked, and of high quality for construction, interior finish, plywood, and many other uses. Ponderosa Pine grows easily from seed in the nursery and in plantings. On good sites, volume growth in young stands is excellent, so that this tree will always be our most important western timber pine.

Leaves and fruit: Its yellow-green needles, 5 to 10 in. long, are borne 3 or occasionally 2 to a bundle, and the foliage stands out stiffly in broom-like tufts from the ends of the stout twigs. The cones, 3 to 5 in. long, are symmetrical in shape, are borne laterally on the branches, and have prickly scales. They fall during the second winter after shedding their seeds, often leaving a few basal scales attached to the branch.

Range: In the Sierra Nevada and in southern Oregon, the Ponderosa Pine is almost as large as the

Sugar Pine, from which it is distinguished by its broad plates of golden-yellow bark. In the bay region, Ponderosa Pine is found on slopes and valleys away from the coast in Sonoma and Napa counties, in a limited area of deep sandy soil near Mount Hermon in Santa Cruz County, and in the Mount Hamilton Range in Santa Clara County. Young trees are seen in gardens, and there are grove plantings in Tilden Park in the Berkeley Hills.

Coulter Pine (*Pinus còulteri*)

This tree is also known as Big-Cone Pine because its heavily armed cones are larger and heavier than the cones of any other pine. It is a hardy species, useful for erosion control under difficult conditions, but is rarely seen as an ornamental.

Leaves and fruit: Coulter Pine closely resembles Ponderosa Pine in habit of growth and in appearance of the needles. However, its needles are usually slightly longer, stiffer, and more bluish green than those of the Ponderosa Pine, and there are always three in a bundle. The yellow-brown cones, usually more than 10 in. long, are armed with heavy curved spurs. Seeds are black and shorter than seed wings.

Range: The best specimens of this drought-resistant, fast-growing tree are found in the mountains of southern California. However, it is also found scattered along upper elevations of the South Coast Ranges, and reaches its northerly limit in a small grove on the north slope of Mount Diablo.

Digger Pine (*Pinus sabiniàna*)

The Digger Pine is sometimes called the Gray Pine because of the smoky, gray-green appearance of its thinly foliaged crown. This is probably the most drought-resistant pine in California. The tough, strong wood has been used mostly for fuel, but is very acceptable for rough construction and is now being used in some quantity for veneer.

Leaves and fruit: The needles, 7 to 13 in. long, are gray-green, slender, and drooping. The heavy, chocolate-brown cones, up to 10 in. long, are sometimes almost as heavily armed as those of the Coulter Pine. Its heavy mottled seeds are longer than the ineffective wing. These seeds, and those of other pines, were important as food for the Indians from which this species takes its common name.

Range: The Digger Pine, with its black-barked trunk that often divides into several stems, is a prominent feature of the foothill grasslands and chaparral. It is of scattered occurrence in the brush fields near Mount Diablo. Because its gray-green foliage contrasts with the dark crowns of other conifers, it is occasionally used as an ornamental.

Knobcone Pine (*Pinus attenuàta*)

The Knobcone Pine is important in erosion control because it grows easily from seed and because of its vigorous growth and ability to withstand drought and sterile soil conditions. Usually found in dense stands, the trees are often stunted, crooked, and much branched from excessive crowding.

Leaves and fruit: The needles, 3 to 6 in. long, are shiny green with a pinkish tinge, and are borne in bundles of threes on slender twigs. The persistent woody cones are borne in whorls, recurved against the trunk or branches, where they cling so tightly as sometimes to be grown over by the growth of the stems.

Range: Knobcone Pine is found in the low-elevation

foothills away from the coast, and often on shallow, sterile soils where few other trees can survive. Typical Knobcone stands can be seen along Empire Grade above Felton in Santa Cruz County, in the Contra Costa Hills above Redwood Canyon, and on Mount Diablo.

Bishop Pine (*Pinus muricàta*)

Usually a tree of moderate size, the Bishop Pine has a dark-green, dense crown. Although it has been used mostly for fuel, its wood is heavy and strong. In Humboldt County, where the tree reached large size in company with Coast Redwood and Douglas Fir, the wood was used for car sills and bridge timbers. The extensive stands of Bishop Pine will undoubtedly be of important future use as Christmas trees and possibly as poles or other forest products.

Leaves and fruit: It has short, stiff needles, 3 to 3½ in. long, in bundles of twos, with a gray-green cast. The unsymmetrical cones, 2½ to 3 in. long, are borne in whorls, and the scales have a sharp spine.

Range: In spite of severe winds, the Bishop Pine

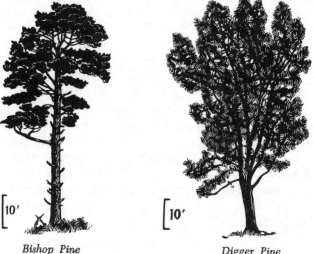

Bishop Pine   Digger Pine

thrives on hills facing the ocean, and is always found within approximately two miles of the coast. There are extensive stands from Marin County north to Trinidad in Humboldt County, and particularly on Point Reyes Peninsula near Inverness and along the Sonoma County coast.

Monterey Pine (*Pinus radiàta*)

It is also called Insignis Pine or Remarkable Pine in areas of mild climate around the world because it is the fastest growing of the more than ninety pine species. It has a dense, dark crown topping a stout trunk with almost black, deeply furrowed bark. The tree is generally of moderate size, but on deep, fertile soils in the Napa and Sonoma valleys planted specimens have reached more than 4½ ft. in diameter and 125 ft. in height in only 60 to 70 years. In Australia, New Zealand, Chile, South Africa, and Spain, trees from many thousands of acres are being used for lumber, plywood, pulp, paper, and other products. In its home area we are content to use it as a windbreak, ornamental, and, in recent years, Christmas tree.

Leaves and fruit: Its dark, blue-green needles, 4 to 4½ in. long, are borne in bundles of threes and twos. The unsymmetrical cones, 4 to 5 in. long, are borne in whorls. Its outer cone scales are thickened and rounded, but do not terminate in a sharp spine, as do the cones of the Bishop Pine.

Range: Monterey Pine grows quickly and easily from seed. Although a native of central California (San Mateo, Monterey, and San Luis Obispo counties), it is in wide use as an ornamental throughout much of the coastal and valley areas as far north as Crescent City. A coastal species of very limited native distribution, it forms a fine forest between Monterey and Carmel and a few miles south. There is a small stand near Cambria, San Luis Obispo County, and it is also found in limited numbers on the Santa Barbara Channel Islands.

Monterey Pine   *Douglas Fir*

Douglas Fir (*Pseudotsuga taxifòlia*)

This tree is of outstanding importance because of its size (8 to 10 ft. in diameter and 275 to 300 ft. in height) and its density on good sites. In volume of standing timber, it is now the leading commercial species in California, Oregon, Washington, and British Columbia.

The bark on young trees is smooth, greenish gray, and marked with blisters containing water-white balsam, which the Indians are said to have used as an antiseptic for wounds. The bark on mature trees is thick, corky, dark brown, and deeply furrowed. When dry, both the wood and bark are excellent fuel. The wood is of fine quality for lumber, interior finish, plywood, pulp, poles, and many other forest products.

Douglas Fir grows easily from seed, is commonly planted as an ornamental, and is perhaps best known as the most widely used Christmas tree throughout the western states.

Leaves and fruit: The short, soft, and dark-green needles are borne singly on tiny stems, and are distributed all around the slender, drooping twigs that grow from stout, sharply rising branches. The dark-red, plump, sharp-pointed, and scaly buds are an important identifying feature, as are the 2½ to 4 in. cones that are carried in a pendent position at the ends of the twigs. The cones ripen in one year, changing from green to brown as they ripen. Since each cone scale is fitted with a leafy, three-pointed bract approximately a half inch longer than the scale, these cones have a very distinctive appearance. Two small, winged seeds under each scale fall when ripe.

Range: One form of the tree has widespread distribution in the Rocky Mountain states. In the bay region it is a constant associate of Coast Redwood, and in the Sierra and Rocky Mountains it grows with Ponderosa Pine, Sugar Pine, Incense Cedar, and other timber species. It is one of the most common trees in all coastal counties from Santa Cruz north.

Grand Fir (*Abies grándis*)

A tall, stately tree, it is also called Lowland White Fir. Its wood is white, soft, and easily worked, but is not durable in the soil and usually considered of second quality. Freshly sawed lumber has a rather unpleasant odor, but this does not persist or prevent its use for rough construction, studding, and fish boxes. Small, symmetrical young trees are excellent Christmas trees, but so far are rarely planted for this purpose or as ornamentals.

Leaves and fruit: Grand Fir is easily distinguished from Douglas Fir by the flat, shiny, dark-green needles that are white beneath. These needles are arranged in flat sprays on horizontal branches that grow in regular whorls. Its plump and barrel-shaped cones, 3 to 5 in. long, mature the first season, and are borne in an erect position on the very upper branches of the tree.

Range: A tree of the northwest coast, Grand Fir is the only one of five true firs native in California that occurs in the bay region, and this one only in northern Sonoma County.

REDWOOD FAMILY (TAXODIACEAE)

Coast Redwood (*Sequoia sémpervirens*)

This is one of the most noteworthy trees in the world for its age (some are more than 2,000 years old), its height (the tallest redwoods exceed 360 ft.), the density of timber on bottomland sites (single acres in Sonoma and Humboldt counties have produced a million board feet of lumber), the rot resistance of its wood (heartwood of many logs left lying in the woods for fifty years or more is still in good condition), and for the majestic beauty of the virgin forest stands.

Redwood bark is thick, soft, and fibrous in texture and reddish brown in color. On old trees it is resistant to fire and, when it is peeled from logs, shredded, and processed, makes an excellent insulation. The uniformly high quality of redwood lumber for construction, interior finish, water and wine tanks, posts, ties, and many other uses is the basis for the thriving lumber industry from Santa Cruz to the Oregon line. An important factor in forest management of about a million acres in the redwood region is the remarkable ability of this tree to reproduce itself both by seeds and from sprouts. Redwood sprouts are a feature of cut-over lands, where they grow rapidly in circles around old stumps, and are also common around standing trees in the forests wherever there is sufficient light. Trees that have had all their branches killed by fire often sprout green foliage from top to bottom, producing what are known on burned areas as "fire columns."

Leaves and fruit: Its flat leaves, bright green at first and dark green when mature, are arranged in two-ranked flat sprays with leaf bases that run down the twig below the point of attachment. Leaves do not fall singly, but the whole twig with its persistent dead leaves falls after two or three years. The globular cones, about ¾ in. in diameter, are borne in clusters on ultimate twigs, turning from green to brown as they ripen. The plump, shield-shaped cone scales shrink apart on drying to release several dark-red, flat, papery seeds that usually fall within 100 feet of the parent tree. Seeds average approximately 100,000 to the pound, and usually 15 to 20 per cent are able to germinate and grow into seedlings. Since many seedlings may die during the first year, it is usual to expect about 5,000 one-year nursery seedlings from a pound of seed. (See pl. 3.)

Range: Originally, redwood grew on 1,250,000 acres within thirty miles of the coast, but usually on slopes and bottomlands protected from the ocean winds. Of this, some 60,000 acres of the finest virgin stands belong to the California state park system. Tree farms, managed for permanent production of forest products, make up much of the balance.

Muir Woods in Marin County, Armstrong Park and

Bohemian Grove in Sonoma County, Memorial Park in San Mateo County, and Big Basin Park and Cowell Park in Santa Cruz County have notable virgin redwood stands.

CYPRESS FAMILY (CUPRESSACEAE)

Gowen Cypress (*Cupressus Goveniàna*)

The Mendocino or Pygmy Cypress, the Sargent Cypress, and the Santa Cruz Cypress are recognized by some as separate species, but here are considered varieties of the Gowen Cypress. These trees exhibit slight differences in cones and leaves.

Leaves and fruit: The tiny scale-like leaves overlap in four rows on the cord-like, slender, squarish branchlets. The backs of the leaves have depressions, but not active pits. The globular cones, ½ to ¾ in. in diameter, mature the second season. Each cone scale is shaped like a shield, culminating in a low, rounded knob. Several small, black or brown winged seeds are borne under each cone scale. (See pl. 3.)

Range: This tree is of scattered occurrence in the Coast Ranges from the "white plains" near Fort Bragg in Mendocino County south to Santa Barbara County. The tiny pygmy forms, which produce many cones when but 1½ to 3 ft. tall, are interesting features of sterile soils and serpentine ridges in Marin, Sonoma, Santa Cruz, and Monterey counties. On good soils, often within a few hundred yards of pygmy trees, are found trees as tall as 75 ft. with thin, fibrous bark and very good tree form. Rarely seen as an ornamental.

Macnab Cypress (*Cupressus macnabiàna*)

This tree is usually much branched and shrubby in form, but some are 40 ft. tall. (See pl. 3.)

Leaves: The foliage is gray-green and more pungently fragrant than that of any other cypress.

Range: An interior northern tree, it grows on dry hills or flats from central Sonoma and Napa counties north to Shasta County.

Monterey Cypress (*Cupressus macrocárpa*)

Although the Monterey Cypress has the most restricted natural range of any California tree, it is included here because it has been widely planted as a hedge, windbreak, and ornamental tree throughout the bay region.

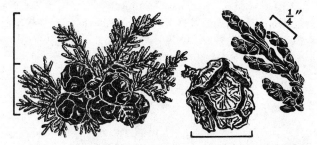

Leaves and fruit: The foliage of dark-green, cord-like twigs has a density and wind resistance that make it an ideal tree for shelter all along the coast. Its somewhat oblong cones, approximately 1½ to 2 in. in diameter, usually have seven pairs of shield-shaped scales that rise to a low, conical point. The irregularly shaped seeds are brown, narrowly winged, and have a white attachment scar at the base.

Although the foliage and cones of Italian Cypress (*Cupressus sémpervirens*), which is widely planted as an ornamental, are very similar to those of the Monterey Cypress, the form of this introduced tree is usually erect and columnar.

Monterey Cypress

Range: Its natural range is limited to two small coastal areas on Cypress Point and Point Lobos in Monterey County. Monterey Cypress is short lived away from the coast, and in recent years has been almost eliminated from interior sections by the spread of Cypress Canker disease and attacks by the Cypress Bark Beetle. Fortunately, the disease and pests are not such serious menaces near the coast or north of the bay.

Incense Cedar (*Libocedrus decúrrens*)

As an ornamental the Incense Cedar often assumes a columnar form, but in the forest its growth is spreading and conical. The bark on young stems is smooth and dark red, but soon thickens, and on mature trees is thick, deep brown, and fibrous. The sapwood is white or cream colored, and the heartwood brown with a spicy, resinous odor. The wood is light in weight, fine grained, easily worked, and takes a fine polish. It splits easily, and is so resistant to rot in the soil that it is widely used for posts and railroad ties. The best quality lumber is used for pencils and cedar chests, but knotty cedar is a favorite wood for interior paneling.

The tree grows easily from seed, and develops a bunchy, fibrous root system that is easily transplanted. The Indians used the tough roots of cedar for fish lines and for tying things together.

Leaves and fruit: The Incense Cedar has flat sprays of foliage on which the scale-like leaves are opposite in pairs, with the leaf bases united with the stem for more than half the leaf length. This characteristic of the leaf bases is called decurrent and gives this species its scientific name. The ¾-inch cones, borne in pendent clusters, become golden yellow when they ripen the first autumn. The cones contain only two pairs of fertile scales with two resinous winged seeds per scale. Trees must be of considerable age before cones are produced. (See pl. 4.)

Range: This tree of the Sierra timber belt grows naturally in the bay region only on the slopes of Mount St. Helena, but is one of the hardiest and most widely planted conifers throughout California. Other cedars are in common use as ornamentals, but none has the decurrent leaves or cones the size and shape of Incense Cedar.

California Juniper (*Juniperus califórnica*)

A small, bushy tree with brown and shreddy bark, the California Juniper is not used as an ornamental (those seen in cultivation are usually from China). It is of interest mainly because of its ability to thrive in the heat and drought of desert hills.

Leaves and fruit: The dull-green leaves are in threes, each with a tiny pit toward the base. The cones ripen as bluish or dark-reddish berries, containing brown, hard-shelled seeds in a dry, sweetish pulp. These occur only on female trees, the male trees bearing tiny pollen conelets.

[31]

Range: The California Juniper ranges from the hills of the Mojave Desert north along the inner Coast Ranges to its northern limit on Mount Diablo.

YEW FAMILY (TAXACEAE)

Western Yew (*Taxus brevifòlia*)

The Western Yew is a small understory tree rarely taller than 40 ft., but some have diameters of 24 in. The trunk is coated with a thin, smooth, reddish bark that peels off in thin shreds. The brownish wood is fine grained, hard, strong, and elastic. It was used by the Indians to make their most powerful bows and is still used by archers, but trees of sufficient size for modern bows are hard to find. The wood is also highly regarded by craftsmen for making cribbage boards, book ends, and lathe-turned wood products.

The columnar, dark-foliaged yew trees commonly seen in lawns and gardens in this area are usually varieties of the famous English Yew (*T. baccata*).

Leaves and fruit: Its leaves resemble those of Coast Redwood, but are darker blue-green above and light yellow-green beneath. The attractive fruits, borne on the under side of sprays on female trees, consist of a single seed set in a succulent, brilliant-red cup or berry. (See pl. 4.)

Range: The Western Yew is usually found growing singly or in small groups in cool, shady canyons from the Santa Cruz Mountains north in the Coast Ranges and at a few locations in the Sierra timber belt.

California Nutmeg (*Torreya califórnica*)

Known also as Torreya or Tumion, it occasionally reaches good size (3 ft. in diameter and 60 ft. in

Sugar Pine

Ponderosa Pine

Coulter Pine

Digger Pine

Plate 1.

Knobcone Pine

Bishop Pine

Monterey Pine

Douglas Fir

Plate 2.

Grand Fir

Coast Redwood

Gowen Cypress

Macnab Cypress

Plate 3.

Incense Cedar

Western Yew

California Nutmeg

California Laurel

Plate 4.

Yellow Willow

Red Willow

Arroyo Willow

Toyon

Plate 5.

Pacific Dogwood

Pacific Red Elder

Giant Chinquapin

Tanoak

Plate 6.

Blue Oak

Oregon Oak

Valley Oak

California Black Oak

Plate 7.

Coast Live Oak

Interior Live Oak

Oracle Oak

Canyon Live Oak

Plate 8.

height) and good forest form. The tree reproduces vigorously from stump sprouts like redwood, but is slow growing. The seeds require a long period of after-ripening before germination takes place, so that many are destroyed by insects or animals. The fibrous bark is thin and brownish, and the wood is fine grained, easily worked, durable in the soil, and of all-around excellent quality. It would have high commercial value if the trees occurred in sufficient quantity to be logged to advantage.

Leaves, flowers, and fruit: The leaves are flat, sharply pointed, stiff, yellow-green on both surfaces, and arranged in two-ranked flat sprays of foliage. Male and female flowers occur on separate trees, the fruit developing as a green, olive-like drupe that becomes purplish when ripe. The large, single seed has inside its shell a white endosperm (food storage tissue) surrounding the tiny embryo. In cross-section this seed resembles the fragrant nutmeg of commerce, but is in no way related to it. (See pl. 4.)

Range: Nowhere abundant, it occurs on lowland flats and along canyon bottoms and hillsides from the Santa Cruz Mountains north through Mendocino County and at scattered points in the Sierra. It makes a handsome ornamental, but is rarely seen in cultivation because of its slow growth.

BROADLEAF TREES

Generally, broadleaf evergreen trees are character-istic of climatic zones in the world where the weather is mild, frosts are few, and snowfall is rare. Deciduous trees are generally found in regions where winters are more severe. However, in the bay region, several species—California Black Oak, Valley Oak, California Buckeye, Bigleaf Maple, Pacific Dogwood, alders, and willows—lose their leaves each fall in spite of the mild weather, whereas Canyon Live Oak is evergreen at elevations in the mountains where there is much snow and severely cold temperatures.

Broadleaf trees have netted veins and the embryo seedling usually has two seed leaves (cotyledons). Their fruits are of many types—single to multiple and flowers may be inconspicuous to very showy and in-complete (lack either sepals, petals, stamens, or pis-til) to complete (with sepals, petals, stamens, and pistil). The flowers may also be imperfect (having only either male or female elements) or perfect (having both male and female elements). When both sexes are on a single tree it is said to be monoecious, but when a tree has flowers of one sex (either male or female) it is said to be dioecious. The leaves are of many kinds and arrangements—simple or compound; broad or narrow bladed; entire or with toothed or lobed margins; long stemmed, short stemmed, or sessile; and either alternate, opposite, or whorled in arrangement. Most of these variations are to be found among the twenty-one broadleaf deciduous and the eleven broadleaf evergreen species native in the bay region.

The wood of broadleaf trees is not resinous and is more complex than that of conifers, containing cells called *vessels* and wood fibers. Since the wood is usually harder than that of softwoods (conifers), broad-leaf trees are often referred to as hardwoods. However, some broadleaf species, such as the willows and cottonwoods, have wood that in density and strength is inferior to that of many of the conifers. In general, the broadleaf trees of this area are not lumber trees because of their much branched, spreading habit of growth or their scattered distribution. They have, therefore, been used mostly for minor forest products (firewood, posts, tannin extract, etc.) and for small woodcraft products (book ends, bowls, lamp-stands, etc.).

BROADLEAF DECIDUOUS TREES

WILLOW FAMILY (SALICACEAE)

The leaves are simple and alternate in arrangement, with leaf-like basal stipules. The male and female flowers, arranged in catkins, are borne on separate trees. The seeds are cottony-winged. Willows (*Salix*): leaves narrow, slender, with short stalks, buds with a single scale and not resinous coated. Poplars *(Populus)*: leaves with expanded blade and long stalk, buds with many scales and often sticky with resin.

The Indians, having no tools, used willow sprouts—stuck in the ground, tied together with roots or withes, and covered with branches, tules, or slabs of bark—for their huts or shelters. (Pl. 5 shows willows.)

Yellow Willow (*Salix lasiándra*)

An attractive streamside tree, the Yellow Willow grows to a height of 50 ft. One-year branchlets are yellow, and the trunk is dark brown and rough.

Leaves: It has long, taper-pointed leaves, up to 7 in. long by 1 in. broad, on leaf-stalks that are ½ in. long,

[43]

warty near the leaf base and subtended by a pair
of prominent, leafy stipules.

Range: Throughout the bay region and elsewhere
in California in suitable habitats.

Red Willow (*Salix laevigàta*)

It is approximately the same size as the Yellow
Willow. The Red Willow's one-year branches are
reddish brown.

Leaves: The leaves are broader near the base with
short-pointed or rounded tips. The ½-inch leaf-stalks
are *not warty,* and the stipules are usually very small
or absent because they fall early.

Range: Throughout the bay region and elsewhere
in California in suitable habitats.

Arroyo Willow (*Salix lasiólepis*)

A smaller tree, up to 35 ft. in height, its bark is smooth
or lightly seamed.

Leaves: It is often called White Willow because its
leaves are green above but white pubescent beneath.
The leaves, 1½ to 5 in. long, are usually *broader above*

the middle, with a short, blunt point, and with entire, rolled-under margins.

Range: Throughout the bay region and elsewhere in California in suitable habitats.

Other willows of this area that are usually smaller and shrubby include: Velvet Willow (*Salix còulteri*), Sandbar Willow (*S. hindsiàna*), Dusky Willow (*S. melanópsis*), Nuttall Willow (*S. scouleriàna*), and Sitka Willow (*S. sitchénsis*). Weeping Willow (*S. babylónica*) and Pussy Willow (*S. díscolor*) are planted as ornamentals.

Fremont Cottonwood (*Poplus frèmonti*)

A handsome tree in cultivation, it becomes 75 to 80 ft. tall and occasionally 4½ to 5 ft. in diameter. It has rarely been sawed into lumber, but is used mainly for temporary fences and for fuel in valley sections where it is often the only species available.

Leaves: It has delta-shaped leaf blades with curved marginal teeth and a stout petiole.

Range: It is typically a tree of streamsides in hot valley and desert areas where its broadly rounded crown supplies very welcome shade. The common cottonwood along streams throughout most of low-land California, it does not associate with redwood and is found in this area in inland valleys, chiefly from Mount Diablo south. In the North Coast Ranges it was found originally only near Cloverdale along the Russian River, but it has been widely planted for shade and windbreaks.

Black Cottonwood (*Populus trichocárpa*)

Often called Western Balsam Poplar because of its sticky, resinous buds, it is the largest of all western poplars, reaching its largest size and greatest com-

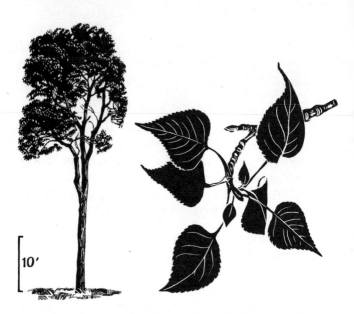

10'

mercial value in the Puget Sound Country. It is smaller in California than it is farther north. The timber stand in this state has been estimated by the Forest Service to be approximately eighty million board feet, but little is cut.

Leaves: Tapered to a slender point, its heart-shaped leaves, usually 5 to 7 in. long, are deep green above and rusty-silvery colored beneath, giving an attractive display of colors in a breeze.

Range: It has a wide distribution along river flats and high valleys in the mountains. Although the Black Cottonwood is not common in the bay region, it is found in Mitchell Canyon, on Mount Diablo, along the Pajaro River, and on both slopes of the Santa Cruz Mountains and south.

Planted poplars in this area include European Silver Poplar (*Populus álba*), Eastern Cottonwood (*P. deltoìdes*), Chinese Poplar (*P. sinensis*), and the

[46]

columnar Lombardy Poplar (*P. nìgra itálica*), which is one of the most widely planted ornamental trees throughout the world.

WALNUT FAMILY (JUGLANDACEAE)

This is an important family of timber trees. The leaves are alternate and compound. Male and female flowers are borne on the same tree in pendent catkins. The few-to-many female flowers are clustered or on a pendent stalk. The fruit is a nut with a hard or succulent husk or a winged nutlet. The family includes Walnuts, Hickories, and Wingnuts.

Hinds Black Walnut (*Juglans hìndsi*)

In contrast with the shrubby Southern California Black Walnut, the Hinds Black Walnut is a large and stately tree. It reaches 75 ft. in height and 4 ft. in diameter, with deeply furrowed, almost black bark and a broadly rounded crown of stout branches. The wood is of excellent quality for carving, interior finish, and furniture. It is used as a root stock on which is grafted the important English Walnut (*J. règia*). (English Walnut, extensively planted in orchards in the Walnut Creek, Santa Clara, and Sonoma valleys, is distinguished by its broad leaflets, usually 5 to 7, and by its smooth, gray bark.) When crossed with Black Walnut (*J. nìgra*) or English Walnut, the hybrids often grow rapidly and produce lumber of excellent grain and figure.

Leaves, flowers, and fruit: The leaves are pinnately compound (feather-like), 7 to 13 in. long, with 11 or more ovate, serrate leaflets that decrease in size from base to tip of the leaf. Leaf arrangement is alternate on stout twigs that may be recognized by the chambered pith and the greenish buds that do not have bud scales. The male flowers are crowded in plump, pendent catkins, 2 to 4 in. long, that fall shortly after pollen is shed. Female flowers develop into globular fruits, approximately 1 in. in diameter, containing the ridged, smooth, hard-shelled nut enclosed in a green pulpy husk that becomes black and powdery at maturity.

Range: This is the only species of the walnut family that is native in the bay region, having been found in a limited area along Walnut Creek in Contra Costa County. It is widely planted in parks and along streets and highways for shade and ornament.

BIRCH FAMILY (BETULACEAE)

The birch family includes six genera of trees and shrubs with simple, alternate leaves, male flowers in long, drooping catkins, and female flowers in short catkins or clusters, some resembling a cone. The fruits are small nuts or winged nutlets. California Hazelnut (*Coerylus rostràta* var. *califórnica*) is a native shrub.

White Alder (*Alnus rhombifòlia*)

Easily recognized by its smooth, gray-mottled trunk, it makes a handsome tree under irrigation and is now frequently planted as a lawn tree. The white wood is neither durable nor strong, but splits easily and makes excellent firewood.

Leaves, flowers, and fruit: The leaves, 2 to 4 in. long by half as broad, have finely toothed edges that

[48]

are *not rolled under*. The drooping catkins of male flowers appear on the trees in December and January, making streamsides attractive during winter. The female flowers develop into woody, cone-like fruits that stay on the tree, but open to release tiny, winged nutlets.

Range: It graces all the inland foothill and mountain streams, but near the coast is replaced by Red Alder. Both species may occupy stream banks in some of the canyons opening into San Francisco Bay.

Red Alder (*Alnus rùbra*)

Also called Oregon Alder, its bark is thin, smooth, and gray-white with mottled patches, and is red within. The white to light-brown wood is moderate in weight and hardness, and of a fine grain resembling maple. An excellent box lumber, it is now used for furniture (chiefly chairs), crates, handles, toys, woodenware novelties, and pulp.

Leaves and fruit: Its leaves are larger and coarser than those of the White Alder, with coarsely toothed margins that are *distinctly rolled under*. The fruits are similar to, but approximately twice the size of, those of the White Alder.

Range: Strictly a coastal species, it is found along

streams entering the ocean in a narrow belt from Santa Barbara County north to British Columbia. It forms fine stands on bottomlands in Marin and Sonoma counties and northward. Although both the White Alder and the Red Alder are relatively short lived, they grow rapidly on moist sites. In the Puget Sound Country, Red Alder has taken over great areas of cut-over lands following fires.

BEECH FAMILY (FAGACEAE)

The male flowers are borne on tiny pendent catkins with thread-like stems. The fruit is an acorn enclosed in, or protruding from, a more or less fringed cup. The ring-porous wood is marked by wide medullary rays, and is very strong and useful.

The bay region has eight tree oaks, evenly divided between deciduous and evergreen species, plus two evergreen chaparral shrubs. Of the deciduous oaks, three are *white oaks* and one is a *black oak*. White oaks are usually recognized by their white to grayish bark, leaf lobes that are not spiny tipped, and acorn shells that are smooth within. Black oaks usually have dark-colored bark, spiny-tipped leaf lobes, and hairy acorn shells. The three white oaks are foothill and valley trees, whereas black oak is a forest associate mostly of Ponderosa Pine. (For oaks, see pl. 7.)

Blue Oak (*Quercus doúglasi*)

Also called Mountain White Oak, it can be recognized by its almost white bark and blue-green foliage. These slow-growing trees are usually of moderate size, but a few reach a height of 75 ft. The wood is heavy, hard, strong, and fine grained. It is an excellent fuel, and Blue Oak fence posts are in wide use in foothill areas.

Leaves and fruit: The leaf shape varies from narrow oblong to rounded oval, the lobes being very shallow; often the margin is almost entire. The leaves, 2 to 3 in. long by half as broad, are coated with fine hairs above. The acorns are plump and broader than the shallow cup, the acorn shell being often coated with a bluish bloom on the outer surface.

Range: A tree of dry foothill areas, it is rarely planted as an ornamental, but deserves wider use in dry regions. Blue Oak will not stand much soil moisture, and old trees are often killed by irrigation of lawns and gardens of foothill homes.

Oregon Oak (*Quercus garryàna*)

The bark is very white, thin, quite smooth, checked into squarish plates, and, in cool, shaded canyon areas, often coated with moss. Oregon Oak has the most useful wood of any western oak, and in the north is used for furniture, veneer, and finish lumber. It makes a long-lasting post and excellent firewood.

Leaves and fruit: The leaves are usually deeply lobed, broader above the middle, dark and shiny green above, and paler and slightly hairy beneath with yellow veins. The first-year acorns, 1 to 1½ in. long and nearly as broad, are plump and seem to bulge from the small, thin cups.

Range: Oregon Oak extends from the Santa Cruz Mountains, where it has limited distribution, through upper elevations of the North Coast Ranges into Oregon and Washington, where it becomes a tree of noble size and great beauty. In California it is usually 2 to 4 ft. in diameter and 40 to 50 ft. in height, although on rocky ridges there are extensive thickets of trees only 8 to 10 ft. tall.

Valley Oak (*Quercus lobàta*)

Called *"Roble"* by the Spanish Californians, this towering, broad-crowned tree often reaches 9 ft. in diameter and more than 100 ft. in height. The hard but brittle wood is little used except for fuel, although in recent years it has been used for keel blocks and rough construction. The tree grows easily and rapidly from seed and makes a fine ornamental for parks, highways, and large gardens.

Leaves and fruit: The deeply and symmetrically lobed leaves, 4 to 5 in. long by half as broad, are deep green above and paler beneath, with a thin coating of short hairs and yellow veins. The long, conical acorns, to 2½ in. long and ¾ in. broad, are dark brown when ripe and fitted with a brown, warty cup approximately ¾ in. deep.

Range: The Valley Oak prefers and grows best in valleys and river flats back from the ocean, and follows stream canyons to elevations of 2,000 ft. or more into the foothills. Noble specimens are to be seen in the valleys of Sonoma, Napa, Contra Costa, and Santa Clara counties, and it formerly occupied large areas in the Great Central Valley.

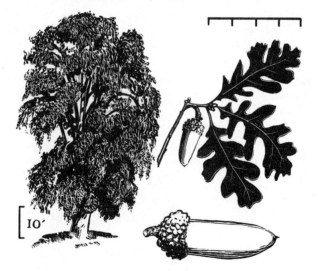

10′

California Black Oak (*Quercus kélloggi*)

A tree of often large and good forest form, it is now being tested as a source of lumber. The wood is hard and heavy and makes a fine fuel.

Leaves and fruit: When the leaves unfold in spring they are an attractive pink or red color and coated with fine hairs. They soon become deep green and shiny above, lighter green beneath, the blades being broad and deeply lobed with spiny points on the lobe ends. They are usually 6 to 7 in. long and 3 to 4 in. broad, but on sprouts and in the shade are often much larger. The acorns are almost globular in shape, 1 in. long, and deeply set in the large, scaly cup.

Range: California Black Oak is a true mountain tree associated with Ponderosa Pine throughout most of its range in California and southern Oregon. In the Coast Ranges it grows with Douglas Fir, Madrone, and Tanoak, and occasionally with Coast Redwood where the stand is not too dense. Thus it has the most extensive range of any California oak.

PLANE TREE FAMILY (PLATANACEAE)

The Plane Tree Family has but a single genus of streamside trees with three species in America and one in southeastern Europe, with a hybrid between *Platanus occidentalis* x *P. orientalis,* which is now one of the most widely planted street and highway trees throughout California. It is called *Platanus acerifòlia* (London Plane Tree). The leaves often resemble those of maple.

Western Sycamore (*Platanus racemòsa*)

The Western Sycamore becomes a very large tree—up to 100 ft. in height and 5 ft. in diameter—with a

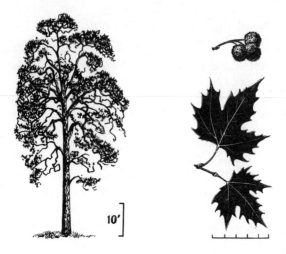

smooth, very beautifully mottled bark and often a leaning and grotesque habit of growth. The wood is light, strong, fine grained with an interesting figure, but is hard to split and is rarely used except for fuel. The Sycamore Canker (*Gnomonia veneta*) is a serious disease during cool, moist weather, often causing complete defoliation and weakening of the trees.

Leaves, flowers, and fruit: It has broad, deeply lobed, light-green velvety leaves that are star shaped, and a leaf-stalk that is expanded at the base to enclose fully the cone-shaped developing bud. Flowers and fruits are in globular clusters distributed along a pendent, slender stem. After ripening, these ball-like fruits remain as a winter feature of the tree, gradually breaking up to release the winged nutlets.

Range: It has wide distribution along rivers and streams and on moist bottomlands from Mount Diablo through the South Coast Ranges to San Diego and up and down the Great Central Valley, but it is absent from valleys of the North Coast Ranges.

For a general discussion of characteristics of the Rose Family, see page 68.

Oregon Crab Apple (*Malus diversifòlia*)

This small deciduous tree is also classified under the scientific name of *Pyrus rivularis* by some authors.

Leaves and flowers: Its serrate, bright-green leaves, 3 to 4 in. long, are coated beneath with rusty hairs. Many of the leaves are three lobed. The white flowers develop into yellowish fruits, ½ in. long, borne 2 to 3 in a cluster, that ripen to a purple-black color.

Range: The Oregon Crab Apple, a native of the northern Pacific Coast, reaches its southern limits in Sonoma and Napa counties. It is nowhere common in California.

HORSE-CHESTNUT FAMILY (HIPPOCASTANACEAE)

Named for the horse-chestnut of Europe, this family includes only two genera. The genus *Aesculus* contains the showy-flowered buckeyes and horse-chestnuts.

California Buckeye (*Aesculus califórnica*)

This is one of the showiest and most beautiful native tree species because of the great masses of creamy-white flowers that appear on the long, erect spikes

during May and June. The tree is often shrubby in dry chaparral areas, but on fertile soils reaches a height of 30 ft. The Indians made flour from the buckeye fruits after extracting the poison. The nectar from buckeye flowers is poisonous to bees.

Leaves, flowers, and fruit: The flowers are often so numerous that they give the rounded crown of the tree the appearance of a great candelabra with thousands of white candles. Its bright-green, palmately compound leaves consist of from five to seven serrulate leaflets that are joined at a single point on a long leaf-stalk. The oppositely arranged leaves appear early in the spring, and soon after flowering turn brown and fall off in August or early September, probably as a means of protecting the tree from drought. Thus, in the fall the bare, smooth-barked trunks make the tree appear dead. The green buckeye pods continue to enlarge even after the leaves fall, and eventually split open to release the large, tough-coated shiny-brown "buckeye" seed.

Range: The California Buckeye is a native of canyon slopes and lowland and foothill areas of the Sierra Nevada and the Coast Ranges of California. Horse-chestnuts and the pink-flowering buckeyes are often planted as street trees and ornamentals throughout the bay region.

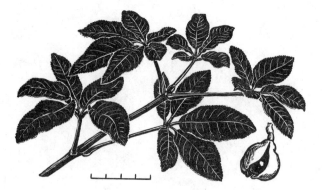

MAPLE FAMILY (ACERACEAE)

This family contains only two genera of opposite-leaved trees and shrubs, most of them with broad-bladed, deeply lobed leaves with long petioles. Flowers are inconspicuous and variable in type, usually blooming in pendent clusters before the leaves, and ripening into a cluster of double-winged fruits. One species has compound leaves. Eastern and European species, which are occasionally planted in California, are fine timber and ornamental trees.

Bigleaf Maple or Oregon Maple
(*Acer macrophýllum*)

Usually found as an understory with other trees, in the open it grows to a height of 90 ft. with a symmetrically rounded crown. It is much planted as a

shade and ornamental tree, for which it is well suited. Young stems have a smooth, gray-green bark, but on old trunks the bark is gray-brown and attractively checked or ridged. The tan-colored wood is hard, close grained, splits and works easily, and is used in the Pacific Northwest for interior finish, veneer, tool handles, furniture, posts, ties, and charcoal.

Leaves, flowers, and fruit: On long leaf-stalks, the

broad-bladed, deeply lobed, opposite leaves are up to 10 in. long—the largest leaves of any American maple. The drooping clusters of yellowish-green flowers on stout, smooth, green-barked twigs make a handsome show before the leaves appear. They ripen into winged fruits (samaras) coated below the 1½ in. long wing with short, stiff hairs. The leaves turn a bright golden color in the fall, making a fine contrast among the dark conifers with which it associates.

Range: It extends from southern California north to British Columbia, and grows along streams and in moist canyons throughout the bay region.

Boxelder (*Acer negúndo*)

The Boxelder is also called Ash-leaved Maple because of its ash-like, compound leaves.

Leaves, flowers, and fruit: The light-green leaves are opposite on smooth-barked twigs that are often coated with a bluish-white bloom. The three leaflets

have doubly serrate margins. The male and female flowers are on different trees. The male flower, on long, slender, thread-like stems, is borne in such vast quantities as to give entire trees a cobwebby appearance. The fruits are reddish when young and coated with fine hairs, but become creamy white when mature, the wings being about ½ in. long.

Range: It is a streamside and bottomland tree throughout this area and, although it is short lived, has been extensively planted in gardens because of its fast growth. The California variety is one of several forms of this tree that has an extensive distribution throughout the United States.

DOGWOOD FAMILY (CORNACEAE)

This family includes several genera of opposite-leaved trees and shrubs, of which the most noteworthy are the flowering dogwoods of the eastern and western United States. These are small to medium sized trees with snowy white or pink flowers, but there are several shrubby dogwoods with less conspicuous flowers that grow along streams.

Pacific Dogwood (*Cornus núttalli*)

This tree, also called Mountain Dogwood, is another of our showy and beautiful western trees. Although it is usually found growing under the shade of timber trees, such as Ponderosa Pine and Douglas Fir, it sometimes becomes a slender tree up to 50 ft. in height. Pacific Dogwood has a smooth, dark, gray-green bark. Its wood is white, heavy, hard, and very fine grained.

Leaves, flowers, and fruit: Its tiny flowers are borne in dense heads above spreading, broad, white bracts that, in May and June, are a notable feature of deep,

[59]

shady woods. The flowers, which appear before the leaves, are greenish cream colored at first, but usually become snowy white when the leaves are about half grown. Borne on short leaf-stalks, the dark-green, opposite leaves, 3 to 5 in. long by half as broad, have rounded or short-pointed tips and entire margins. In autumn they make a brilliant show as they turn various shades of red or pink before they fall. The scarlet-colored fruit, approximately ½ in. across, is a rounded head of clustered seeds. (See pl. 6.)

Range: Pacific Dogwood is usually found in shady woods, such as those in Yosemite Valley and at points along the Redwood Highway. It is not abundant in this area, but there are some trees on Howell Mountain in Napa County, on the slopes of Mount St. Helena, and in the Santa Cruz Mountains. It is occasionally planted as an ornamental, but grows slowly and succeeds best in partial shade.

OLIVE AND ASH FAMILY (OLEACEAE)

This family includes approximately 20 genera of opposite-leaved trees and shrubs, many of which are handsome ornamentals. The most important, however, are the Common Olive (*Olea europea*), extensively grown for its edible fruit and oil, and the ashes (*Fraxinus* sp.), many of which are large and useful timber trees.

Oregon Ash (*Fraxinus oregòna*) or (*F. latifòlia*)

A moisture-loving and usually medium-sized tree, it occasionally reaches a height of 80 ft. and a diameter of 3 ft. on the best sites. The wood, like that of other ashes, is brownish and rather coarse grained, but is hard and strong and has many uses, including interior finish, furniture, tool handles, oars, and veneer.

Leaves, flowers, and fruit: Its compound leaves occur in opposite arrangement on stout, smooth twigs. The leaflets are light green and, except for the terminal one, without stalks. Their margins are entire or toothed above the middle. There are usually 5 to 7 leaflets, the entire leaf measuring 6 to 12 in. in length. The inconspicuous flowers appear in clusters just before the leaves in spring, male and female occurring on different trees. The winged fruits, shaped like small canoe paddles, occur in drooping clusters.

Range: It has an extensive range from San Diego to British Columbia, with best development in Oregon. Oregon Ash is too scattered in occurrence in California to be of commercial importance, and is rarely used as an ornamental. It is widely distributed along water courses in this area, but only occasionally is found in groves on moist flats of river valleys.

Arizona Ash (*F. velùtina*) from the southwest is frequently planted.

HONEYSUCKLE FAMILY (CAPRIFOLIACEAE)

This family includes thirteen genera of opposite-leaved shrubs or small trees, many of which are attractive ornamentals with perfect flowers and simple or pinnate, compound leaves.

Blueberry Elder (*Sambucus gláuca*)

Also called Blue Elderberry, it is a small tree, up to 30 ft. in height and 1½ ft. in diameter. Many of these trees are very attractive both in flower and fruiting stages. Elderberry stems may be recognized by their large, soft pith.

Leaves, flowers, and fruit: It has opposite, compound leaves with 5 to 7 shiny green leaflets 1 to 4 in. long, with finely toothed margins. The small white flowers occur in a flat-topped cluster, and ripen into small bluish berries with a white bloom. These are often used in making jelly and wine and are very attractive to birds.

Range: The tree form is only of scattered occurrence, being replaced over much of its range by the bush form, which consists of several straggly stems from a single root, some stems dying back and being replaced by rapidly growing sprout growth. It is, only occasionally planted as an ornamental.

Pacific Red Elder (*Sambucus callicárpa*)

Also called Red Elderberry, it is an attractive tree of no commercial value.

Leaves, flowers, and fruit: This tree is very similar to the Blueberry Elder except for the berries, which are bright red and occur in ovate clusters 2 to 3 in. long. (See pl. 6.)

Range: The Pacific Red Elder is a shrub over much of its extensive range in the Sierra Nevada north and east, but becomes a tree 25 ft. tall on bottomlands near Inverness, Marin County, and northward along the coast.

BROADLEAF EVERGREEN TREES

SWEETGALE or BAYBERRY FAMILY (MYRICACEAE)

These are small trees or shrubs with simple, alternate, finely serrate leaves; unisexual flowers in catkins; and waxy, grayish, or purple fruits.

Pacific Bayberry (*Myrica califórnica*)

Also called California Waxmyrtle, it is a shrub or small tree (to 35 ft.). The wax from the Atlantic Coast species (*M. cerífera*) is used in the manufacture of bayberry candles.

Leaves and fruit: It has shiny, lustrous-green, narrow leaves and greenish-to-purplish, wax-coated berries.

Range: The Pacific Bayberry is an attractive ornamental that succeeds well on sterile soils and severely windy locations. It is found on slopes and in canyons near the ocean throughout this area and north to Puget Sound. There are handsome, smooth-barked trees along the Los Gatos–Santa Cruz Highway near Camp Evers.

BEECH FAMILY (FAGACEAE)

For a discussion of general characteristics of oaks, see page 50. (For oaks, see pls. 6–8.)

Coast Live Oak (*Quercus agrifòlia*)

Also called Encina or California Live Oak, it gave the City of Oakland its name. Extensive groves of this oak once grew where the City of Oakland now is. The Coast Live Oak has broadly rounded crowns, massive trunks encased in smooth, gray-green plates of bark, and masses of holly-like foliage borne on wide-spreading, sturdy branches. Although it is usually of moderate size, occasional specimens of 10 ft. diameter are

found., The wood is heavy, hard, and strong, but the spreading form of the tree precludes its use for lumber. It makes excellent fuel and is widely used in the manufacture of charcoal.

Leaves, flowers, and fruit: The leaves are shiny green on both sides, but slightly darker on the upper surface, and on the under side it is usual to find tufts of tan-colored, downy hairs in the axils of the veins. They have margins with regularly spaced, spiny teeth, and are usually convex upward, like the bowl of a teaspoon turned upside down. The leaves persist through the winter, but on many trees are almost completely shed just before the new foliage appears. The clustered, thread-like male flowers give the trees a cobwebby appearance during late March and April, but these soon fall, leaving the tiny female flowers to develop by autumn into small, slenderly pointed acorns deeply set in a fringed cup. The acorn shell is coated within with felt-like hairs, the outer surface being marked by vertical color bands.

Range: These impressive trees give distinctive beauty to rolling hills, canyons, and north-facing slopes of the Coast Ranges from Mendocino County to Mexico, at elevations up to approximately 3,500 ft. The Coast Live Oak is the commonest native tree throughout the bay region.

Interior Live Oak (*Quercus wislizèni*)

Also known as Highland Live Oak, this is a medium-sized black oak tree with dark, burrowed bark.

Leaves and fruit: Shiny green on both sides, the leaves are flat and leathery, with margins usually marked by stout, widely spaced teeth. The slender acorns ripen the second year.

Range: A tree of the dry ridges and foothills east

of the typical range of Coast Live Oak, it associates with Blue Oak, Digger Pine, and chaparral shrubs.

Oracle Oak (*Quercus mórehus*)

The Oracle Oak is an evergreen black oak, with smooth (except on old stems), dark, ashy-gray bark. It rarely exceeds 35 ft. in height.

Leaves and fruit: The leaves—broad, leathery, shiny lobed, and tipped with spines—resemble those of the California Black Oak. However, since the leaves are persistent through the winter until the new foliage appears, it is classed as a live oak. The acorns mature the second autumn and are enclosed for approximately one-third of their length in a reddish-brown cup.

Range: Scattered individuals occur with other oaks, and the species is generally considered a natural hybrid of Interior Live Oak and California Black Oak.

Canyon Live Oak (*Quercus chrysólepis*)

Also known as Maul Oak or Iron Oak because its heavy and hard wood was used for the heads of mauls by the pioneers. When fully grown, it is the most massive of western oaks. One specimen in Boquet Canyon, Los Angeles County, had a diameter of 11 ft. and a huge, wide-spreading crown of sturdy branches. Canyon Live Oak is a white oak with light-colored, vertically striated bark.

Leaves and fruit: Its variable leaves are dark, shiny green above and a dull, lead color beneath. Newly developing foliage and acorns are golden yellow. The leaf margins vary from plain to holly-like, often on the same twig. Acorns mature the second autumn, protruding from a thick, golden-tinged, turban-shaped cup. The inner surface of the shell is hairy.

Range: Maul Oak is usually found at elevations above the range of Coast Live Oak. Large specimens are found on Mount Tamalpais, Mount Diablo, and in the Santa Cruz Mountains, but shrubby forms are not uncommon in the chaparral.

Tanoak (*Lithocarpus densiflòra*)

Not a true oak, Tanoak (or Tanbark Oak) becomes a tall forest tree of good form. Its trunk is coated with a thick, smooth, gray-green bark that for years has been an important source of tannin for the western leather industry. The wood is dense and hard, with an attractive grain, but is not durable in the soil. It will no doubt be more fully used in the future because the tree sprouts vigorously from the stump.

Leaves, flowers, and fruit: Its flowers are borne in clustered, erect spikes resembling those of chestnut. The coarsely toothed leaves also resemble those of the chestnut. The fruit, however, is a plump acorn that matures during the second autumn in a shallow cup fringed with spreading scales. The oblong leaves, 3 to 5 in. long, and the ultimate twigs and the acorns are coated with dense, wooly hairs.

Range: Tanoaks are widely distributed in the redwood region and back from the coast where they associate with Madrone, California Laurel, and Douglas Fir. Many cut-over lands in the North Coast Ranges are coming up to dense stands of this species.

Giant Chinquapin (*Castanopsis chrysophýlla*)

This is the western tree that most closely resembles the chestnut trees of the eastern United States and the Mediterranean, because the small, brown nuts are set in a spiny bur like the chestnut. The fibrous bark is dull brown, reddish inside, and divided into thick, rounded ridges. Its wood is light and strong but, because it is very difficult to season, is rarely used except for fuel.

Leaves: The leaves, which taper both to base and tip, are leathery in texture, have entire margins, are dark green above, and are coated with fine golden hairs beneath.

Range: On good sites in the North Coast Ranges it is a towering forest tree more than 100 ft. in height and as much as 6 ft. in diameter. In our area it is usually much smaller, and there are shrubby forms in the chaparral. There are typical tree specimens approximately 50 ft. tall on Mount Tamalpais and, with Bishop Pine, on Point Reyes Peninsula.

LAUREL FAMILY (LAURACEAE)

This is a large family of trees and shrubs, mostly with alternate, simple, and *aromatic* leaves, and drupe or berry-like fruits, some of which are edible. It includes the Grecian Laurel (*Laurus nóbilis*), famed in history as a symbol of victory; Camphor Tree (*Cinnamomum camphòra*), commonly used as a street tree in the bay region; and the edible Avocado (*Persea americàna*).

California Laurel (*Umbellularia califórnica*)

This tree is also known as Pepperwood, Bay Tree, and Oregon Myrtle. The California Laurel is highly variable in size. The wood is heavy, hard, fine grained, and exceedingly strong. In Oregon there is an industry making bowls, lampstands, and other souvenirs from selected, finely figured burls of laurel.

[67]

The leaves, like those of the Grecian Laurel, are often used to give flavor in cooking.

Leaves, flowers, and fruit: Its entire, leathery, dark-green leaves, 3 to 5 in. long, have entire margins, wedge-shaped bases, and short-pointed tips. They are alternate in arrangement, shiny above, dull beneath, and when crushed have a strong, peppery aromatic fragrance that is their most notable characteristic. The tiny, clustered, yellow-green flowers bloom in winter or early spring and ripen into oval fruits resembling the olive, the thin flesh turning from green to purple and becoming succulent when mature. (See pl. 4.)

Range: It is very widely distributed throughout this entire region, from streamsides and fertile valleys where it reaches massive proportions to rocky ridges exposed to severe ocean winds where it is shrubby and only a few feet in height.

ROSE FAMILY (ROSACEAE)

This family includes approximately 100 genera of herbs, shrubs, and trees typically with five-parted flowers. Many of these plants have edible fruits and are of great value to man. Many are trees, shrubs, or vines of outstanding ornamental value. Apples, peaches, pears, plumbs, cherries, berries, and hawthorns, spiraeas, and roses are among the most important. Three small trees are native here.

Toyon or Christmas Berry (*Photinia arbutifòlia*)

This is one of the best-known California species because of the widespread use of sprays of its glossy foliage and clusters of its bright-red berries for Christmas decoration. It is also called California Holly. Some authors classify Toyon under the generic name *Heteromeles*.

Leaves, flowers, and fruit: Its dark-green leaves, approximately 4 in. long, have finely toothed margins, and are short stalked and alternately arranged. The flowers appear in June and July as white drooping clusters. The bright-red berries ripen in November or early December. (See pl. 5.)

Range: Though usually a shrub on hillsides and in chaparral areas, it becomes an attractive tree on deep lowland soils throughout this area. It is in wide use as a planted ornamental.

HEATH FAMILY (ERICACEAE)

This is a very large family of hardwood trees and shrubs with simple leaves and often showy flowers. It includes many fine ornamentals, such as Scotch Heather, Trailing Arbutus, Manzanita, Strawberry Tree, Rhododendron, and the huckleberries.

Madrone (*Arbutus ménziesi*)

The Madrone's broad, shining evergreen foliage and smooth, green-tan and red bark add greatly to the beauty of any area in which it is found. There are notably large Madrone specimens—including the massive Council Madrone near Ettersburg in Humboldt County, beneath which Indian tribes are said to have held their councils—but in our area the trees are usually of moderate size. It grows in association with Tanoak, Douglas Fir, and sometimes with Coast Redwood. Madrone sprouts vigorously after fires or logging operations and, with Tanoak, is an important constituent of second-growth on logged lands in the North Coast Ranges. Its fine-grained, heavy, and hard wood takes a fine polish and makes an excellent hardwood floor. It is an attractive ornamental species, but is not easy to transplant, even as a small seedling. In recent years a fungus leaf-spot disease has caused serious defoliation of Madrones in several parts of its range.

Leaves, flowers, and fruit: Its glossy, light-green leaves, 3 to 6 in. long by 1 to 3 in. broad, have entire or finely toothed margins, and are alternate in arrangement on smooth, greenish-tan stems. The flowers are small, white, waxy bells hanging in dense clusters at the twig ends. These ripen into orange-red berries, ½ in. in diameter, which when mature are eagerly sought by birds.

Range: This strikingly handsome tree ranges from British Columbia to southern California, and grows in association with Tanoak, Douglas Fir, and sometimes with Coast Redwood.

SUGGESTED REFERENCES

McMinn, Howard E., and Evelyn Maino. *An Illustrated Manual of Pacific Coast Trees.* Berkeley: University of California Press, 1935.

Holt, Vesta. *Key to Wild Flowers, Ferns, Trees and Shrubs of Northern California.* Palo Alto: National Press, 1955.

Sudworth, George B. *Forest Trees of the Pacific Slope.* Washington, D.C.: U.S. Govt. Printing Office, 1908.

U.S. Dept. of Agriculture. *Trees: The Yearbook of Agriculture.* Washington, D.C.: U.S. Govt. Printing Office, 1949.

CHECK LIST OF BAY REGION
NATIVE TREES

PINE FAMILY (PINACEAE)
Sugar Pine (*Pinus lambertiàna*), p. 18, pl. 1.
Knobcone Pine (*Pinus attenuàta*), p. 21, pl. 2.
Digger Pine (*Pinus sabiniàna*), p. 20, pl. 1.
Coulter Pine (*Pinus còulteri*), p. 20, pl. 1.
Ponderosa Pine (*Pinus ponderòsa*), p. 19, pl. 1.
Monterey Pine (*Pinus radiàta*), p. 23, pl. 2.
Bishop Pine (*Pinus muricàta*), p. 22, pl. 2.
Douglas Fir (*Pseudotsuga taxifòlia*), p. 24, pl. 2.
Grand Fir (*Abies grándis*), p. 25, pl. 3.

REDWOOD FAMILY (TAXODIACEAE)
Coast Redwood (*Sequoia sémpervirens*), p. 26, pl. 3.

CYPRESS FAMILY (CUPRESSACEAE)
Incense Cedar (*Libocedrus decúrrens*), p. 30, pl. 4.
Gowen Cypress (*Cupressus goveniàna*), p. 28, pl. 3.
Monterey Cypress (*Cupressus macrocárpa*), p. 29.
Macnab Cypress (*Cupressus macnabiàna*), p. 28, pl. 3.
California Juniper (*Juniperus califórnica*), p. 31.

YEW FAMILY (TAXACEAE)
Western Yew (*Taxus ḅrevifòlia*), p. 32, pl. 4.
California Nutmeg (*Torreya califórnica*), p. 32, pl. 4.

WILLOW FAMILY (SALICACEAE)
Yellow Willow (*Salix lasiándra*), p. 43, pl. 5.
Red Willow (*Salix laevigàta*), p. 44, pl. 5.
Arroyo Willow (*Salix lasiólepis*), p. 44.
Fremont Cottonwood (*Populus frèmonti*), p. 45.
Black Cottonwood (*Populus trichocárpa*), p. 45.

WALNUT FAMILY (JUGLANDACEAE)
Hinds Black Walnut (*Juglans hìndsi*), p. 47.

SWEETGALE or BAYBERRY FAMILY (MYRICACEAE)
Pacific Bayberry (*Myrica califórnica*), p. 62.

BIRCH FAMILY (BETULACEAE)
White Alder (*Alnus rhombifòlia*), p. 48.
Red Alder (*Alnus rùbra*), p. 49.

BEECH FAMILY (FAGACEAE)
Coast Live Oak (*Quercus agrifòlia*), p. 63, pl. 8.
Interior Live Oak (*Quercus wizlizèni*), p. 64, pl. 8.
Oracle Oak (*Quercus mórehus*), p. 65, pl. 8.
Canyon Live Oak (*Quercus chrysólepis*), p. 65, pl. 8.
Blue Oak (*Quercus doúglasi*), p. 50, pl. 7.
Oregon Oak (*Quercus garryàna*), p. 51, pl. 7.
Valley Oak (*Quercus lobàta*), p. 52, pl. 7.
California Black Oak (*Quercus kélloggi*), p. 53, pl. 7.
Tanoak (*Lithocarpus densiflòra*), p. 66, pl. 6.
Giant Chinquapin (*Castanopsis chrysophýlla*), p. 66, pl. 6.

PLANE TREE FAMILY (PLATANACEAE)
Western Sycamore (*Platanus racemòsa*), p. 53.

LAUREL FAMILY (LAURACEAE)
California Laurel (*Umbellularia califórnica*), p. 67, pl. 4.

ROSE FAMILY (ROSACEAE)
Toyon (*Photinia arbutifòlia*), p. 69, pl. 5.
Oregon Crab Apple (*Malus diversifòlia*), p. 55.

HORSE-CHESTNUT FAMILY (HIPPOCASTANACEAE)
California Buckeye (*Aesculus califórnica*), p. 55.

MAPLE FAMILY (ACERACEAE)
Bigleaf Maple (*Acer macrophýllum*), p. 57.
Boxelder (*Acer negúndo*), p. 58.

DOGWOOD FAMILY (CORNACEAE)
Pacific Dogwood (*Cornus núttalli*), p. 59.

HEATH FAMILY (ERICACEAE)
Madrone (*Arbutus ménziesi*), p. 69.

OLIVE and ASH FAMILY (OLEACEAE)
Oregon Ash (*Fraxinus oregòna* or *F. Latifòlia*), p. 60.

HONEYSUCKLE FAMILY (CAPRIFOLIACEAE)
Blueberry Elder (*Sambucus gláuca*), p. 61.
Pacific Red Elder (*Sambucus callicárpa*), p. 62.